Row, row, row your boat,
Gently down the stream.
Merrily, merrily, merrily, merrily,
Life is but a dream.

 *Sit on the floor facing each other in pairs, feet touching
and holding hands, and sway backwards and forwards.*

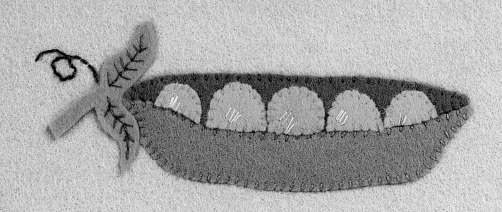

For Joannie and Johnny with love – C. B.

Barefoot Books, 3 Bow Street, 3rd Floor, Cambridge, MA 02138

Compiled by Mary Finch. Illustrations copyright © 2001 by Clare Beaton
The moral right of Clare Beaton to be identified as the illustrator of this work has been asserted

This book was typeset in Celestia Antiqua 18 on 24 point. The illustrations were prepared in
antique fabrics and felt with braid, buttons, beads and assorted bric-a-brac. Graphic design by
Judy Linard, England. Color transparencies by Jonathan Fisher Photography, England. Color
separation by Grafiscan, Italy. Printed and bound in Singapore by Tien Wah Press (Pte) Ltd.
This book is printed on 100% acid-free paper.

3 5 7 9 8 6 1

Cataloguing-in-Publication Data

Beaton, Clare
    Playtime rhymes for little people / Clare Beaton.
[47] p. : col. ill. ; 26 cm.
Summary: Nursery rhymes with instructions for accompanying body movements.
ISBN: 1-84148-425-3
1. Counting-out rhymes. 2. Nursery rhymes. I. Title.
398.8 —dc21   2001   AC CIP

PLAYTIME RHYMES FOR LITTLE PEOPLE

Clare Beaton

Barefoot Books
Celebrating Art and Story

CONTENTS

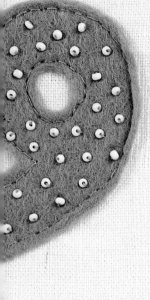

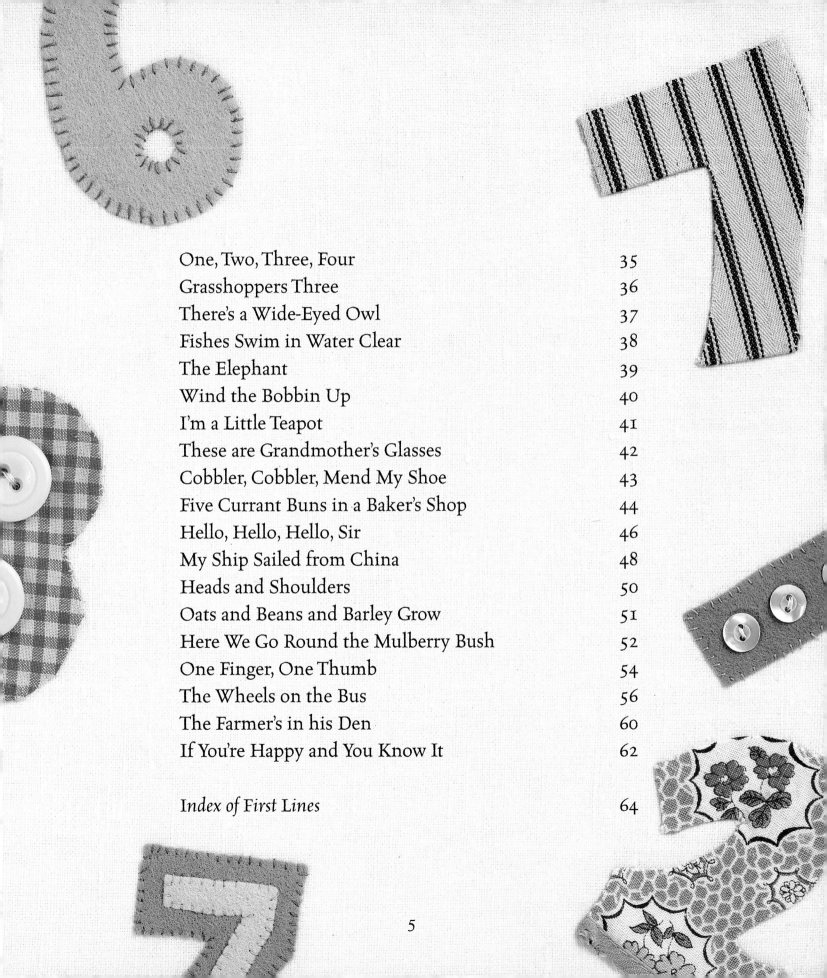

HERE ARE THE LADY'S KNIVES AND FORKS

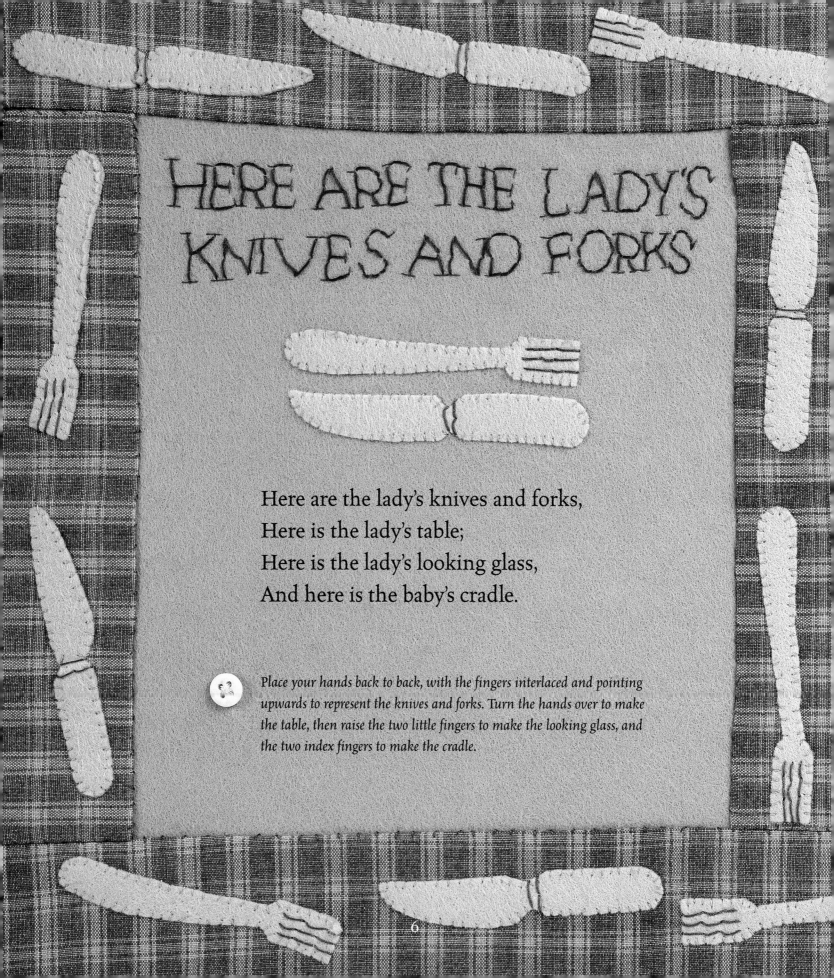

Here are the lady's knives and forks,
Here is the lady's table;
Here is the lady's looking glass,
And here is the baby's cradle.

Place your hands back to back, with the fingers interlaced and pointing upwards to represent the knives and forks. Turn the hands over to make the table, then raise the two little fingers to make the looking glass, and the two index fingers to make the cradle.

SLOWLY, SLOWLY

Slowly, slowly, very slowly,
Creeps the garden snail.
Slowly, slowly, very slowly,
Up the wooden rail.

Quickly, quickly, very quickly,
Runs the little mouse.
Quickly, quickly, very quickly,
Round about the house.

*Walk your hand very slowly up the baby's tummy in the
first verse, and tickle the baby all through the second.*

ROUND AND ROUND THE GARDEN

Round and round the garden,
Runs the teddy bear.
One step, two steps,
Tickle you under there.

*Run your index finger around the baby's palm, then
jump the fingers up the arm and tickle under the chin.*

9

THIS IS THE
MAN THAT
BROKE
THE
BARN

This is the man that broke the barn,
This is the man that stole the corn,
This is the man that stood and saw,
This is the man that ran away,
And this is the man that paid for all.

Wiggle each of the baby's toes at each line.

10

11

HANKY PANKY

Down by the banks of the hanky panky,
Where the bullfrogs jump from bank to banky,
With a hip, hop, hippity hop,
Jump off the lilypad,
And kerplop!

Bounce up and down to the rhythm with the child on your knee.
On "bank to banky" lift the child from knee to knee. Stop all movement
on "jump" and let the child fall backwards on "kerplop!".

13

THIS IS THE WAY THE LADIES RIDE

This is the way the ladies ride,
Nim, nim, nim, nim;
This is the way the gentlemen ride,
Trim, trim, trim, trim;
This is the way the farmers ride,
Trot, trot, trot, trot;
This is the way the huntsmen ride,
A-gallop, a-gallop, a-gallop, a-gallop;
This is the way the plowboys ride,
Hobbledy-gee, hobbledy-gee,
And down into the ditch.

Sit the child on your lap, facing you and holding your hands.
Jog your knees slowly and then more rapidly, according to the
sense of each verse. On the last line, tip the child backwards
down your legs while still holding hands.

A FARMER WENT TROTTING

A farmer went trotting upon his gray mare,
     Bumpety, bumpety, bump!
With his daughter behind him so rosy and fair,
     Lumpety, lumpety, lump!

A raven cried, "Croak!" and they all tumbled down,
     Bumpety, bumpety, bump!
The mare broke her knees and the farmer his crown,
     Lumpety, lumpety, lump!

The mischievous raven flew laughing away,
     Bumpety, bumpety, bump!
And vowed he would serve them the same the next day,
     Lumpety, lumpety, lump!

*Sit the child on your lap, facing you and holding your hands. Jog your knees
up and down, tipping the child backwards down your legs and up again when
everyone tumbles down.*

TWO LITTLE DICKY BIRDS

Two little dicky birds,
Sitting on a wall;
One named Peter,
One named Paul.

Fly away, Peter!
Fly away, Paul!
Come back, Peter!
Come back, Paul!

*Hold up the index fingers of each hand, and fold them down
as the birds fly away. Straighten them again as the birds return.*

HERE IS THE CHURCH

Here is the church, and here is the steeple,
Open the doors, and here are the people.
Here is the parson going upstairs,
And here is the parson a-saying his prayers.

Interlace the fingers with the knuckles uppermost. Point the index fingers to represent the steeple and open the thumbs as the doors. Turn the hands inside with the fingers still interlaced, and wriggle the fingers to represent the people. As the parson goes upstairs, place the hands back to back and intertwine the fingers one by one. Finally, bring the palms together so that your thumb appears in a pulpit of knotted hands.

19

TOMMY THUMB

Tommy Thumb, Tommy Thumb,
Where are you?
Here I am, here I am,
How do you do?

Peter Pointer, Peter Pointer,
Where are you?
Here I am, here I am,
How do you do?

Toby Tall, Toby Tall,
Where are you?
Here I am, here I am,
How do you do?

Ruby Red, Ruby Red,
Where are you?
Here I am, here I am,
How do you do?

Baby Small, Baby Small,
Where are you?
Here I am, here I am,
How do you do?

*Wriggle each finger in turn,
starting with the thumb.*

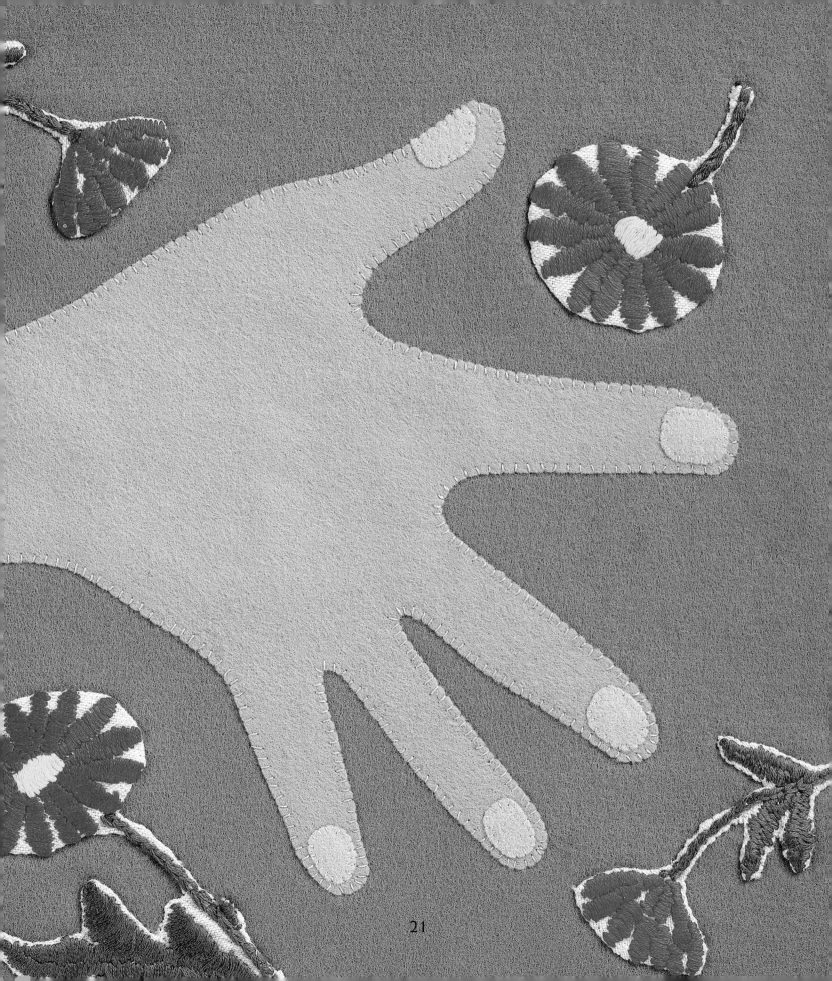

FIVE LITTLE PEAS

Five little peas in a pea-pod pressed,
One grew, two grew, and so did all the rest.
They grew and they grew and they did not stop,
Until one day the pod went pop!

*Clench the fingers of one hand, and open them out slowly.
On the third line stretch all the fingers, and on "pop" clap both
hands together.*

INCY WINCY SPIDER

Incy wincy spider climbed up the water spout.
Down came the rain and washed the spider out.
Out came the sun and dried up all the rain,
Incy wincy spider climbed up the spout again.

*Touch index fingers and thumbs together in turn to make the movements
of the spider. Raise the hands and lower them, wriggling your
fingers to indicate the rain. Make a circular movement with the
hands for the sun, and then repeat the spider action.*

23

I HAD A LITTLE CHERRY STONE

I had a little cherry stone
And put it in the ground.
And when next year I went to look,
A tiny shoot I found.

The shoot grew upwards day by day
And soon became a tree.
I picked the rosy cherries then,
And ate them for my tea.

Use the right thumb and forefinger to plant the cherry stone in the left hand. Clench the left fist with the right forefinger poking up as the shoot. Then use both hands to represent the growing shoot, keep your right hand upright as the tree and pick the cherries with your left hand.

My hat it has three corners,
Three corners has my hat.
If it did not have three corners,
It would not be my hat.

Point first to yourself, then to your head and then indicate the shape of the hat.

25

FIVE LITTLE DUCKS

Five little ducks went swimming one day,
Over the pond and far away.
Mother Duck said, "Quack, quack, quack!"
But only four little ducks came back.

Four little ducks went swimming one day,
Over the pond and far away.
Mother Duck said, "Quack, quack, quack!"
But only three little ducks came back.

Three little ducks went swimming one day,
Over the pond and far away.
Mother Duck said, "Quack, quack, quack!"
But only two little ducks came back.

Two little ducks went swimming one day,
Over the pond and far away.
Mother Duck said, "Quack, quack, quack!"
But only one little duck came back.

One little duck went swimming one day,
Over the pond and far away.
Mother Duck said, "Quack, quack, quack!"
And five little ducks came swimming right back.

Wriggle the fingers of your hand to represent the ducks swimming.

INTERY, MINTERY

Intery, mintery, cutery, corn,
Apple seed and briar thorn;
Wire, briar, limber lock,
Five geese in a flock,
Sit and sing by a spring,
O-U-T and in again.

This is a counting-out rhyme.

ONERY, TWOERY

Onery, Twoery,
Ziccary zan,
Hollow bone, crack-a-bone,
Ninery, ten.
Spit, spot,
It must be done,
Twiddlum, twaddlum,
Twenty-one.

This is a counting-out rhyme.

ONE POTATO, TWO POTATO

One potato, two potato,
Three potato, four.
Five potato, six potato,
Seven potato, more.
O-U-T spells out,
So out you must go,
Because the king and queen say so.

This is a counting-out rhyme. Each child holds both hands in a balled fist, and the counter goes round in a circle, touching the fists on the numbers and, for the last three lines, on each word. On "out" the hand is put behind the child's back and the count starts again, until only one child is left.

Hinx, minx, the old witch winks,
The fat begins to fry.
Nobody at home but jumping Joan,
Father, mother and I.
Stick, stock, stone dead,
Blind man can't see,
Every knave will have a slave,
You or I must be HE.

This is a counting-out rhyme.

31

ONE, TWO, BUCKLE MY SHOE

One, two,
Buckle my shoe;

Three, four,
Knock at the door;

Five, six,
Pick up sticks;

Seven, eight,
Lay them straight;

Nine, ten,
A big fat hen;

Eleven, twelve,
Dig and delve;

Thirteen, fourteen,
Maids a-courting;

Fifteen, sixteen,
Maids in the kitchen;

Seventeen, eighteen,
Maids in waiting;

Nineteen, twenty,
My plate's empty.

This rhyme is to encourage children to clean their plates. Each pair of numbers represents a mouthful.

TINKER, TAILOR

SOLDIER

SAILOR

TAILOR

RICH MAN

TINKER

Tinker,
Tailor,
Soldier,
Sailor,
Rich man,
Poor man,
Beggarman,
Thief.

*This is a fortune-telling rhyme
used when counting the stones
in a fruit pie.*

THIEF

BEGGARMAN

POOR MAN

One, two, three, four,
Jenny at the cottage door.
Five, six, seven, eight,
Counting cherries on her plate.

This is a counting rhyme.

GRASSHOPPERS THREE

Grasshoppers three a-fiddling went,
Hey, ho, never be still.
They paid no money towards their rent,
But all day long with their elbows bent,
They fiddled a tune called "Rilloby, rilloby,"
Fiddled a tune called "Rilloby, rill."

This is a marching song. On the first two lines make the motions of playing a fiddle. On the third line open the arms wide, on the fourth put your hands on your hips, and then continue fiddling for the last two lines.

THERE'S A WIDE-EYED OWL

There's a wide-eyed owl,
With a pointed nose.
He has pointed ears,
And claws for toes.
He sits in a tree,
And looks at you,
Then flaps his wings and says,
"Tu-whit, tu-whoo!"

Point to the different parts of your body and finish by
flapping your arms and shouting "Tu-whit, tu-whoo".

FISHES SWIM IN WATER CLEAR

Fishes swim in water clear,
Birds fly up into the air;
Serpents creep along the ground,
Boys and girls run round and round.

Dip your hands up and down to represent the fishes; flap your arms
to represent the birds; lie down and creep on the floor to represent the
serpents, then jump up for the final line.

THE ELEPHANT

The elephant goes like this and that,
He's terribly big and he's terribly fat;
He has no fingers, he has no toes,
But goodness gracious, what a nose!

*Link your hands and sway your arms to represent the elephant
moving; spread your arms wide to show his size; fold up your
fingers to show that he has no fingers or toes; then link your
hands again and raise your arms to represent his trunk.*

WIND THE BOBBIN UP

Wind the bobbin up, wind the bobbin up,
Pull, pull, clap, clap, clap.
Wind the bobbin up, wind the bobbin up,
Pull, pull, clap, clap, clap.
Point to the ceiling, point to the floor,
Point to the window, point to the door,
Clap your hands together, one, two, three,
And put your hands upon your knee.

*Roll hands round each other, and then make a pulling motion
as if stretching elastic. Clap hands, and then point to the
appropriate place as it is mentioned.*

I'M A LITTLE TEAPOT

I'm a little teapot, short and stout,
Here's my handle, here's my spout.
When I see a teacup hear me shout,
Lift me up and pour me out.

Hold one arm out sideways as the spout, and place the other one on your hip as a handle. Tip to the side of the outstretched arm to pour the tea.

THESE ARE GRANDMOTHER'S GLASSES

These are Grandmother's glasses,
This is Grandmother's hat.
Grandmother claps her hands like this,
And puts them in her lap.

These are Grandfather's glasses,
This is Grandfather's hat.
Grandfather folds his arms like this,
And has a little nap.

Use your thumb and forefingers to make the shape of glasses and hold them to your eyes; put your hands on top of your head for the hat, then clap your hands and put them in your lap. Repeat for Grandfather, but fold your hands under your cheek to show him falling asleep.

COBBLER COBBLER, MEND MY SHOE

Cobbler, cobbler, mend my shoe,
Get it done by half-past two.
Half-past two is far too late,
Get it done by half-past eight.

Sit on the floor, with both legs stretched out. On the first and second lines, hammer both fists on knees. On the third and fourth lines, drum both feet on the floor.

FIVE CURRANT BUNS

Five currant buns in a baker's shop,
Round and fat with a cherry on the top.
Along came a boy with a penny one day,
Bought a currant bun and took it right away.

Four currant buns in a baker's shop,
Round and fat with a cherry on the top.
Along came a boy with a penny one day,
Bought a currant bun and took it right away.

Three currant buns in a baker's shop,
Round and fat with a cherry on the top.
Along came a boy with a penny one day,
Bought a currant bun and took it right away.

Two currant buns in a baker's shop,
Round and fat with a cherry on the top.
Along came a boy with a penny one day,
Bought a currant bun and took it right away.

One currant bun in a baker's shop,
Round and fat with a cherry on the top.
Along came a boy with a penny one day,
Bought a currant bun and took it right away.

IN A BAKER'S SHOP

This can be played with fingers, or with a
group of children in a circle. One child is the
boy with the penny, the others are the currant
buns. The first child leads one child from the
circle each time s/he buys a currant bun. The
first number should correspond with the
number of children playing.

"Hello, hello, hello, sir,
Meet me at the grocer."
"No, sir."
"Why, sir?"
"Because I have a cold, sir."
"Where did you get your cold, sir?"
"At the North Pole, sir."
"What were you doing there, sir?"
"Counting polar bears, sir."
"Let me hear you sneeze, sir."
"Kachoo, kachoo, kachoo, sir."

*This is a skipping song with a steady rhythm until the words "Kachoo, kachoo, kachoo",
which are skipped in double time.*

47

My ship sailed from China with a cargo of tea,
All laden with presents for you and for me.
It brought me a fan, just imagine my bliss,
When I fanned myself gently like this, like this.

My ship sailed from China with a cargo of tea,
All laden with presents for you and for me.
It brought me two fans, just imagine my bliss,
When I fanned myself gently like this, like this.

My ship sailed from China with a cargo of tea,
All laden with presents for you and for me.
It brought me three fans, just imagine my bliss,
When I fanned myself gently like this, like this.

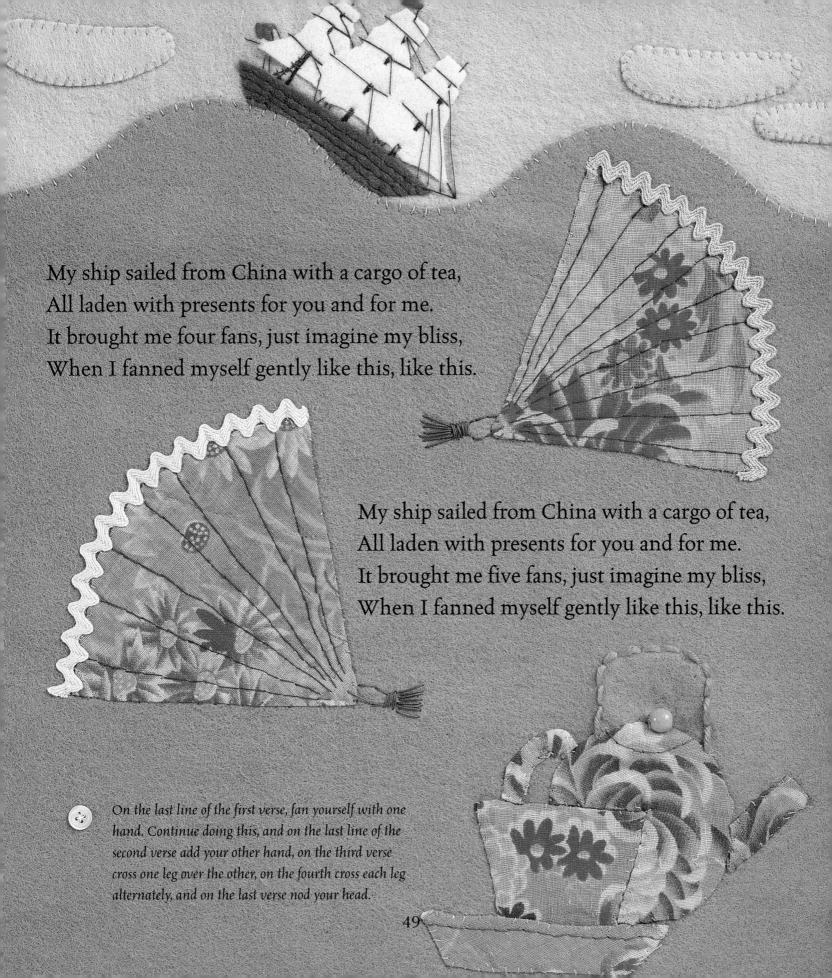

My ship sailed from China with a cargo of tea,
All laden with presents for you and for me.
It brought me four fans, just imagine my bliss,
When I fanned myself gently like this, like this.

My ship sailed from China with a cargo of tea,
All laden with presents for you and for me.
It brought me five fans, just imagine my bliss,
When I fanned myself gently like this, like this.

On the last line of the first verse, fan yourself with one hand. Continue doing this, and on the last line of the second verse add your other hand, on the third verse cross one leg over the other, on the fourth cross each leg alternately, and on the last verse nod your head.

HEADS AND SHOULDERS

HEAD

EARS

EYES

NOSE

MOUTH

SHOULDERS

Heads and shoulders, knees and toes,
Knees and toes,
Heads and shoulders, knees and toes,
Knees and toes,
And eyes and ears and mouth and nose,
Heads and shoulders, knees and toes,
Knees and toes.

Touch each part of the body in turn. A variant is to sing the rhyme over and over again, leaving out the word "head" the first time, but still touching it, the "head" and the "shoulders" the second time etc. until eventually the whole rhyme is mimed.

TOES

KNEES

OATS AND BEANS AND BARLEY GROW

Oats and beans and barley grow,
Oats and beans and barley grow,
But you or I nor anyone know,
How oats and beans and barley grow.

First the farmer sows his seed,
Then he stands and takes his ease,
Stamps his feet and claps his hands,
And turns around to view the land.

*Skip around in a ring for the first verse. For the second,
stand still and mime the actions.*

HERE WE GO ROUND THE MULBERRY BUSH

Here we go round the mulberry bush,
The mulberry bush, the mulberry bush,
Here we go round the mulberry bush,
On a cold and frosty morning.

This is the way we clean our teeth,
Clean our teeth, clean our teeth,
This is the way we clean our teeth,
On a cold and frosty morning.

This is the way we brush our hair,
Brush our hair, brush our hair,
This is the way we brush our hair,
On a cold and frosty morning.

*Skip around in a ring for the first verse, then
mime the actions to the next two. Add any
other actions you like.*

53

ONE FINGER, ONE THUMB

One finger, one thumb, keep moving,
One finger, one thumb, keep moving,
One finger, one thumb, keep moving,
We'll all be merry and bright.

One finger, one thumb, one arm, keep moving,
One finger, one thumb, one arm, keep moving,
One finger, one thumb, one arm, keep moving,
We'll all be merry and bright.

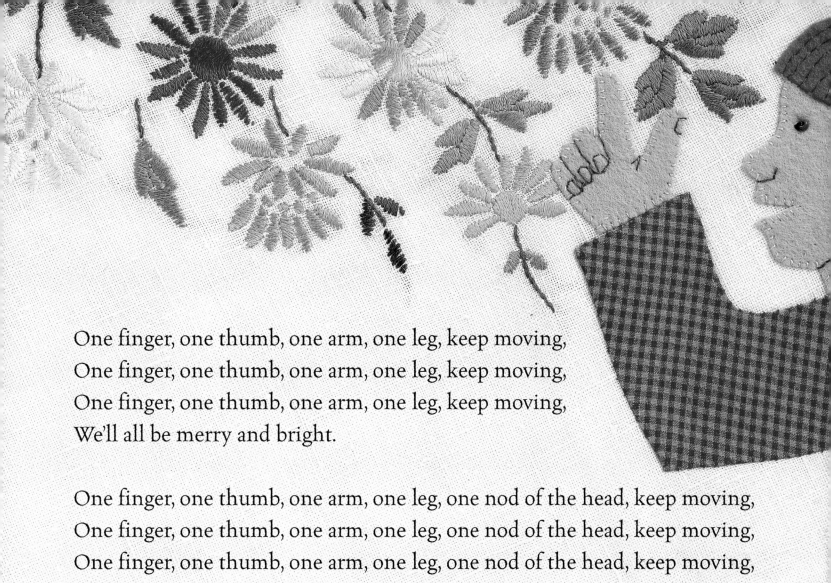

One finger, one thumb, one arm, one leg, keep moving,
One finger, one thumb, one arm, one leg, keep moving,
One finger, one thumb, one arm, one leg, keep moving,
We'll all be merry and bright.

One finger, one thumb, one arm, one leg, one nod of the head, keep moving,
One finger, one thumb, one arm, one leg, one nod of the head, keep moving,
One finger, one thumb, one arm, one leg, one nod of the head, keep moving,
We'll all be merry and bright.

Hold up each part of the body as it is mentioned and keep wriggling it.

THE WHEELS ON THE BUS

The wheels on the bus go round and round;
Round and round; round and round;
The wheels on the bus go round and round;
All day long.

The wipers on the bus go swish, swish, swish;
Swish, swish, swish; swish, swish, swish;
The wipers on the bus go swish, swish, swish;
All day long.

The horn on the bus goes beep, beep, beep!
Beep, beep, beep! Beep, beep, beep!
The horn on the bus goes beep, beep, beep!
All day long.

The conductor on the bus goes, "Tickets, please!
Tickets, please! Tickets, please!"
The conductor on the bus goes, "Tickets, please!"
All day long.

The daddies on the bus go nod, nod, nod;
Nod, nod, nod; nod, nod, nod;
The daddies on the bus go nod, nod, nod;
All day long.

The mommies on the bus go chatter, chatter, chatter;
Chatter, chatter, chatter; chatter, chatter, chatter;
The mommies on the bus go chatter, chatter, chatter;
All day long.

The children on the bus go bounce, bounce, bounce;
Bounce, bounce, bounce; bounce, bounce, bounce;
The children on the bus go bounce, bounce, bounce;
All day long.

*Mime appropriate actions for each verse, ending with the children
bouncing up and down in their places.*

59

THE FARMER'S IN HIS DEN

The farmer's in his den,
The farmer's in his den,
E ... I ... E ... I,
The farmer's in his den.

The farmer wants a wife,
The farmer wants a wife,
E ... I ... E ... I,
The farmer wants a wife.

The wife wants a child,
The wife wants a child,
E ... I ... E ... I,
The wife wants a child.

The child wants a nurse,
The child wants a nurse,
E ... I ... E ... I,
The child wants a nurse.

The nurse wants a dog,
The nurse wants a dog,
E ... I ... E ... I,
The nurse wants a dog.

We all pat the dog,
We all pat the dog,
E ... I ... E ... I,
We all pat the dog.

*Hold hands in a circle with one child in the middle as the
farmer. The children skip around the farmer for the first verse,
then he chooses a wife. The sequence is repeated until the last
verse when all the children pat the dog.*

IF YOU'RE HAPPY AND YOU KNOW IT

If you're happy and you know it, clap your hands,
If you're happy and you know it, clap your hands,
If you're happy and you know it,
And you really want to show it,
If you're happy and you know it, clap your hands.

If you're happy and you know it, stamp your feet,
If you're happy and you know it, stamp your feet,
If you're happy and you know it,
And you really want to show it,
If you're happy and you know it, stamp your feet.

If you're happy and you know it, shout "We are!"
If you're happy and you know it, shout "We are!"
If you're happy and you know it,
And you really want to show it,
If you're happy and you know it, shout "We are!"

Clap, stamp, shout.

WE ARE!

WE ARE!

63

INDEX OF FIRST LINES